Crimp! On-By!!

The True Story of a Most Unlikely Iditarod Lead Dog

As told to Liz Parrish and Jan Kelley
Designed & Illustrated by Agi Palinay

Life Through Dogs LLC
Fort Klamath, Oregon

© 2009 Liz Parrish and Jan Kelley

All rights reserved. No part of this book may be reproduced in any form or by any electronic or mechanical means, including information storage and retrieval systems, without written permission from the publisher. Written permission is not needed for brief quotations in reviews provided that copies of such reviews are sent to the author.

Printed in the United States of America

Book Manufactured By:
United Graphics
2916 Marshall Ave.
P.O. Box 559
Mattoon, IL 61938-0559

Manufacturing Job Number: 191519
Production Date September 2009

First Edition 2009

Current printing
1

Parrish, Liz and Kelley, Jan

ISBN: 978-0-9841254-0-1

Library of Congress Control Number: 2009906208

Cover, interior illustrations and book design by Agi Palinay

Life Through Dogs LLC
P.O. Box 498
Fort Klamath, OR 97626
541-892-3639
www.lifethroughdogs.com

Introduction

Crimp overcame incredible adversity and odds just to be alive. The idea that he could become a working sled dog and run all the way to Nome seemed about as likely as being able to run to the moon.

I never intended to raise and train Crimp as a sled dog. His nose was crushed and his jaw broken by a bite from an older puppy at just four weeks of age. When I met him three weeks later, he still struggled to eat and breathe. It was a huge disappointment that he was "damaged goods" because he was one of the few male puppies at the kennel that year. His father was a multiple-time Iditarod leader and finisher, and except for his injury, Crimp had the body, lineage and head to follow in his footsteps.

Crimp never gave up his will to live. He kept eating, overcame an infection from the injury, and healed quickly. Because being a sled dog seemed out of the question, I brought Crimp home to be a pet and to provide puppy company for his sister, Sinclair.

However, I forgot to tell Crimp he couldn't be a sled dog. He was a goofball and a rambunctious house pet, but once he discovered running in harness, nothing else mattered.

Crimp loves making friends, loves eating, loves bounding through the meadow for the pure joy of running—yet he will ONLY bark for his harness and the chance to GO!

Crimp shows time and again that he knows who he is and what his destiny is…and nothing will stand in his way!

Liz Parrish

Many thanks belong to:

Jamie
For throwing in Crimp as part of the deal

All the fans of Briar's Patch Sled Dogs
For your enthusiasm, interest, donations and support

Running Y Ranch Readers and Writers Group
For your unwavering encouragement and advocacy

Peggy and Elaine
For making it all possible

Briar
For being my first husky and starting the dream

To everyone who believed in me and gave me a chance, and to my buddies and teammates—

Let's GO!

Crimp

Hi! My name is Crimp!

I am an Alaskan husky, and I like to run around and play with my friends. My favorite times are when we are put in harness together. Then we become a sled dog team.

There is one day in particular I will never forget:

March 1, 2008.

That was the first day of the 2008 Iditarod Race. For the next two weeks, we wore our harnesses, we ran and we pulled and we camped out along the trail.

Wow! What a fun time we had! And here is the best part of my story—

On the very first day, at the start of the race, **I was the LEAD dog! ME!!**

I never, ever dreamed something so special could happen in my life.

But it did!!!

This is my story!

Did You Know?

- *The Iditarod Sled Dog Race is run every March in Alaska from Willow to Nome, a distance of over 1,100 miles.*
- *In 2008, 96 teams started the race, and 78 teams finished.*
- *Teams enter with 16 dogs and one musher who drives the dog team.*
- *The trail goes over mountains, through forests, across long stretches of sea ice, and down frozen rivers.*
- *Teams travel around the clock, alternating between running and resting, traveling through 18 checkpoints on their way to the finish line at Nome.*
- *For more information: www.iditarod.com*

PUPPYHOOD

I was born in Minnesota, and I had a great time playing with all the other puppies in our pen at the kennel.

We yipped and yapped, chased each other, jumped and rolled around together.

Did You Know?

- *Baby sled dogs are raised with their brothers and sisters in a pen.*
- *They stay with their litter until they are about four months old.*
- *While the puppies are in the pen they learn to run and explore and play with other dogs.*
- *Puppies learn most of their social skills during their first year. It is important they are around other dogs, puppies and people to learn good doggie manners.*

But one day something bad happened.

I saw some older puppies on the other side of the fence.

Because I was curious, I went over there and poked my nose through the fence.

I just wanted to say,

HI!

Then one of those older puppies bit my nose HARD!!

OUCH!!!

I still have a dent in my nose from that bite. My nose made me different from all the other dogs.

The worst part, though, was I was afraid to be around any dogs, except for my sister, Sinclair.

I became a shy puppy and I made sure I stayed close to Sinclair all of the time.

One day I heard everybody barking because someone new arrived. That person was Liz, and she was there to pick out some puppies to be part of her sled dog team.

Liz was kind and gentle. She hugged and petted all of us.

Sinclair let Liz know that she really wanted to be one of the puppies to be chosen.

Sinclair followed Liz around and even crawled through small holes in the fence to stay close to her.

Finally, Liz said,

"OK, Sinclair, you can come with me to be on my team."

Of course, no one thought I could be on a sled dog team. I was scared and shy. I snorted and snuffled as I breathed or ate or slept because of the dent in my nose.

To some people, my nose made me look like I was sneering and not at all friendly.

But everyone agreed it would be good for my sister, Sinclair, if I went along to keep her company. So, when Liz bought Sinclair, I was thrown in as part of the deal.

Then Liz knelt down next to me and took a close look at my face.

"In honor of your special nose, I will name you Crimp."

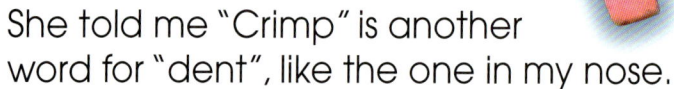

She told me "Crimp" is another word for "dent", like the one in my nose.

I loved my special name, and I was so happy Liz made me a part of her family!

From then on, I called her my Mom Liz.

MOM LIZ

A NEW HOME

When it was time for us to leave our home in Minnesota, Mom Liz loaded each of us into a dog box to travel across the country to Oregon. That's where Mom Liz lived and had her own kennel for the puppies she was training to be sled dogs.

Did You Know?

- Sled dogs travel by vehicle in special compartments called dog boxes.
- Dog boxes are either on or in a truck or a trailer designed especially for the dogs and all their gear.
- Each dog box has soft straw in it for the dogs to rest comfortably.
- The dogs love their boxes and are excited to get in. Travel in the dog boxes means adventure!

I was a scrawny little puppy and I wasn't nearly as pretty as my sister. But looks didn't matter to Mom Liz. She let me live in the house with her other pets.

She gave us all food and water and toys. Every day, she reminded me that I was a very special part of her family.

One day, Mom Liz dressed me up as a Biker Dude for Halloween. I kind of liked everyone saying how cute I looked. And making Mom Liz happy made me happy!

I grew fast, and I was always ready to eat. Mom Liz offered me a pan of bird seed once, and I gobbled it up before I realized what it was.

Bird seed covered my nose and lips and I waited for the next course, while Mom Liz laughed so hard, she cried.

So then Mom Liz had nicknames for me like "Goofball" and "Snorkle Snorffle."

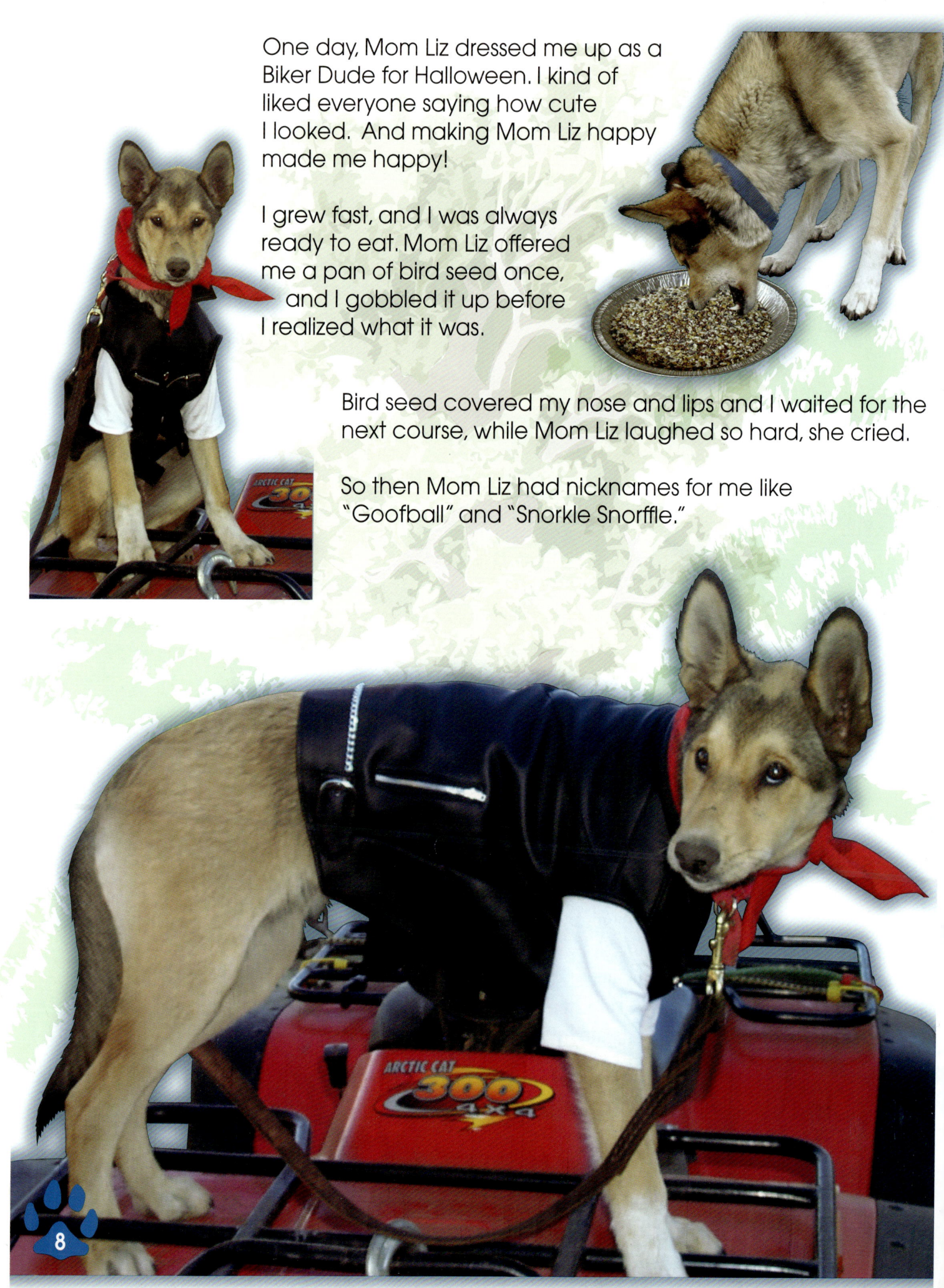

While I lived in the house, I got to sleep on the chairs and the sofa and the bed. I thought it was pretty neat to be a house dog.

One night I learned I could breathe easier and more quietly when I lay on my back.

But the first time I did that, Mom Liz woke up in the middle of the night and was scared.

"I can't hear Crimp!" she cried.

Mom Liz bolted down the stairs to see if I was OK.

I was sound asleep, and just fine.

As I grew up, I had a great time running all around the house and back yard with the other house pets.

UPSTAIRS!

DOWNSTAIRS!

JUMP ON THE BED!

JUMP OFF THE DECK!

OOPS...

I BROKE MY TOE!!

Mom Liz took me to a nice vet who put a splint on my foot and wrapped it all up. The bandage on my foot felt kind of funny, but I forgot about it when I got doggie cookies.

YUM!

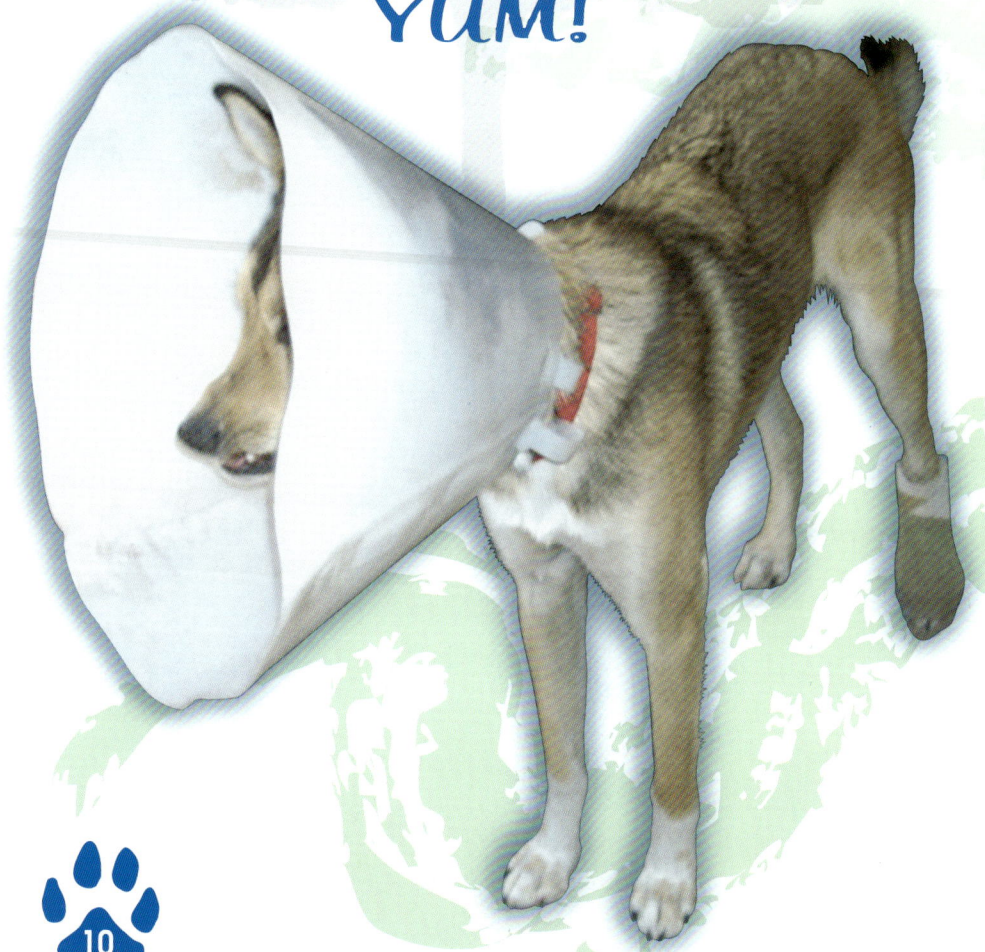

Did You Know?

- *Veterinarians are doctors for animals.*
- *The nickname for veterinarian is "vet."*
- *Vets are good partners who help you take the best care of your animals.*
- *All pets need check-ups and shots to keep them healthy.*

My broken toe did not slow me down at all. I had to wear a special collar over my head so I couldn't chew on my bandage, but in no time I figured out how to push my way through doors and around obstacles.

The next day I was off and running around the house and back yard again, thumping along with the splint on my foot. Mom Liz had a new nickname for me, "Thumper."

It wasn't long until my toe was all better.

At least, we thought it was.

During the time I was a house dog, Mom Liz was so loving and the other house pets were so friendly, I wasn't scared or shy any more.

And, I kept growing and growing until I was as big and strong as the sled dogs in the kennel.

Still, I guess we were all surprised when I decided that I wanted to get to know the other dogs and be more like them!

BECOMING A SLED DOG

After my foot was better, Mom Liz took me along with her to the yard where the sled dogs lived. For a while, I sat outside the gate and just watched while she fed and played with them.

But I was bigger now, and braver too. One day, I ran right into their yard and started making friends.

When Mom Liz saw that, she said, **"Crimp, if it will make you happy, you can move into the yard with your new friends."**

I loved being with the sled dogs. And I found out that actually, I was one of them. I felt at home!

One day, Mom Liz came into the dog yard with an ATV and a bunch of harnesses for some of the sled dogs.

WHAT WERE THEY DOING?

The other sled dogs barked with excitement while Mom Liz put on their harnesses and hooked them to a line attached to the front of the ATV. Then Mom Liz jumped on and started the engine.

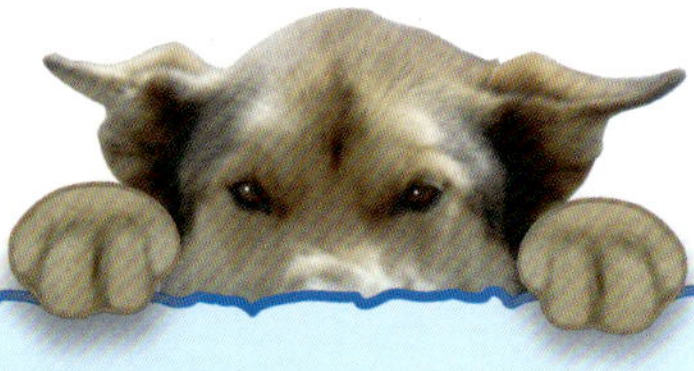

Did You Know?
- Dogs learn by DOING. They need to be exposed to lots of different experiences and environments so they are comfortable with all of them.
- Sled dogs learn to pull ATVs (4-wheeled all-terrain vehicles, also called quads) or carts before they graduate to sleds on snow.
- They train on dirt trails when it is cool enough for them to work each fall.
- Fall training is important to teach the dogs commands, build muscle and endurance, and teach them they can pull in a wide variety of conditions.

"Let's go!" she shouted, and they all started pulling.

From where I was, left behind back in the yard, it sure looked like they were having **FUN!**

HEY! I barked. **WHAT ABOUT ME? I WANT TO PLAY WITH THE OTHER DOGS, TOO!**

And I barked and barked each time I saw Mom Liz and my sister Sinclair and the other sled dogs having such a good time pulling the ATV.

Mom Liz tried to explain to me that I couldn't go with them because I was special. For one thing, sled dogs must breathe well so they don't get too hot as they run.

For another thing, they must use all four legs and feet when they pull.

But I had a dent in my nose, and I had broken my toe.

Mom Liz wanted to make sure I wouldn't do anything that could hurt me.

No matter what she said, I just kept barking.

I WANT TO GO!

I barked and barked, and barked some more.

I REALLY WANT TO GO, TOO!

I CAN DO IT!!

I KNOW I CAN!!!

Did You Know?

• Sled dogs want to pull so much, the musher watches to make sure they don't work too hard.
• The dogs cool off by panting, so they have to be able to breathe through both their nose and their mouth.
• A dog that doesn't get very hot while pulling is called a cool running dog. Crimp would have been a cool running dog except for his nose injury.

Mom Liz petted me and tried to make me quiet down, but I would not stop barking.

I kept barking because I knew I was meant to be a sled dog.

I could feel it in my heart, and nothing would stop me from achieving my destiny.

I CAN!!! I CAN!!! I CAN!!!

Finally, Mom Liz realized I was not going to give up. *"OK, Crimp, I will let you go with the team whenever it is cold outside, but only on short trips."*

She thought that I would not get too hot if I ran while the air was cool, even if the dent in my nose meant I didn't breathe perfectly. And a little pulling would not hurt the toe I had broken.

I was so excited the day Mom Liz let me go along with the other sled dogs for my first adventure pulling!

She put on our harnesses and hooked us up in a line. After that, we barked and jumped while Mom Liz got on the ATV.

When Mom Liz shifted into gear and released the brake, we started to run and pull, and the ATV with Mom Liz on board followed along behind us.

WOW...
SO THIS IS WHAT SLED DOGS DO!

Did You Know?

- *Just like some dogs want to chase balls, sled dogs want to pull and see what's down the trail.*
- *This instinct has been bred into them for generations.*
- *The positions in front of the team are called leaders or lead dogs.*
- *The positions in the back of the team are called wheel dogs.*
- *The dogs in the middle are all called team dogs.*

TRAINING AND RACING

Now I knew why sled dogs get so excited each time they wear their harnesses. What they are going to do is **FUN**!

Every chance I got, I showed Mom Liz I could be a sled dog. Mom Liz called it training, but my teammates and I just enjoyed running and pulling. I would jump and wiggle and bark each time it seemed like we were going to get out on the trail.

All I wanted to do was

GO!

Mom Liz cheered us along, saying,

"Everybody pull!" As we went down the trail she shouted, *"Gee!"* or *"Haw!"* and sometimes, *"On-by!"*

I began to understand that Mom Liz was giving us commands. More than anything, I wanted to do what she asked. I figured out **"Gee"** means turn right, and **"Haw"** means turn left. My favorite command was **"On-by,"** which means keep doing what you are doing no matter what!

Did You Know?

- Sled dog commands are the same as commands used for horses and oxen.
- A sled dog's least favorite command is "Whoa!" The only way to stop the team is to use a brake.
- Mushers NEVER say "Mush" to get the team to go. Some commands that are used are "Hike!", "Alright!" and "Let's Go!"

It was so much **FUN** being a part of a team! I had a great time learning how to be a sled dog. At the same time, Mom Liz was learning how to be a musher. Mom Liz and all of us sled dogs taught each other how to travel by dog team.

Often that meant we tried new things...

One day, Mom Liz put me up in front of the rest of the team as a lead dog. All of the other dogs followed ME! And you know what? Mom Liz and I found out that I was especially good at being a lead dog.

Mom Liz was beaming. **"Crimp, I am so proud of you!"**

That was the day I started to fulfill my true destiny.

I AM CRIMP!

I AM AN ALASKAN HUSKY!

I AM A SLED DOG!

I AM A LEADER!

For the next four years, I ran with the team in lots of different places. We pulled sleds and ATVs through snow and swamps and mud holes. We practiced eating and resting, no matter what time of the day or night. The most important lesson we learned was to trust that Mom Liz would never tell us to do anything that we couldn't do or would hurt us.

I trusted Mom Liz totally, and she trusted me. And I discovered Mom Liz had a dream.

Her dream was to be a musher in the famous Iditarod Sled Dog Race with a sled dog team she trained herself. Her team would run through the wilderness across Alaska. They would be so good they would complete the whole, long Iditarod race.

Together, Mom Liz and I realized my destiny to be a sled dog could fulfill a part of her dream to be a musher in the biggest race of all!

Did You Know?

- *Sled dogs need lots of food to be able to pull hard, stay warm and maintain good coats.*
- *The most important parts of their diet are high quality dog kibble, protein, and fat.*
- *During a distance race or hard training, a sled dog can burn up to 12,000 calories a day. That is the same as a person eating 40 cheeseburgers!*
- *The dogs train hard to learn to eat and rest whenever they can, so they keep their energy replenished.*

LET'S GO! I barked.

One day, we had a big surprise. Instead of going out for another run, Mom Liz loaded us into our dog boxes.

I knew we were on our way to a special adventure.

Did You Know?

• There are many different types of sled dog races.
• Sprint races are usually short trails, with different classes determined by the number of dogs on the team. For example, a 6-dog team will run 6 miles.
• Mid-distance races are 14 to 400 miles long with a team of 6 to 12 dogs.
• Marathon or long distance races are over 500 miles long, typically for teams of 12 to 16 dogs.

I was right! We traveled to a place where we were running our first distance race. We ran 135 miles in this competition against other sled dog teams.

At the last rest stop I kept on resting like Mom Liz wanted us to, long after all the other dogs got up and ready to go.

The checkpoint judge and helpers all thought I wasn't going to run. But when Mom Liz stepped on the runners and shouted **"Let's go!"**...

I jumped right up and pulled hard.

Mom Liz had a big smile on her face, and I was happy to be on the trail again!

We ran 200, 300, even 350 mile races in all sorts of conditions and weather.

At times it was hot and sunny, and we had to slow down.

Often we ran at night because it was cooler and rested during the day.

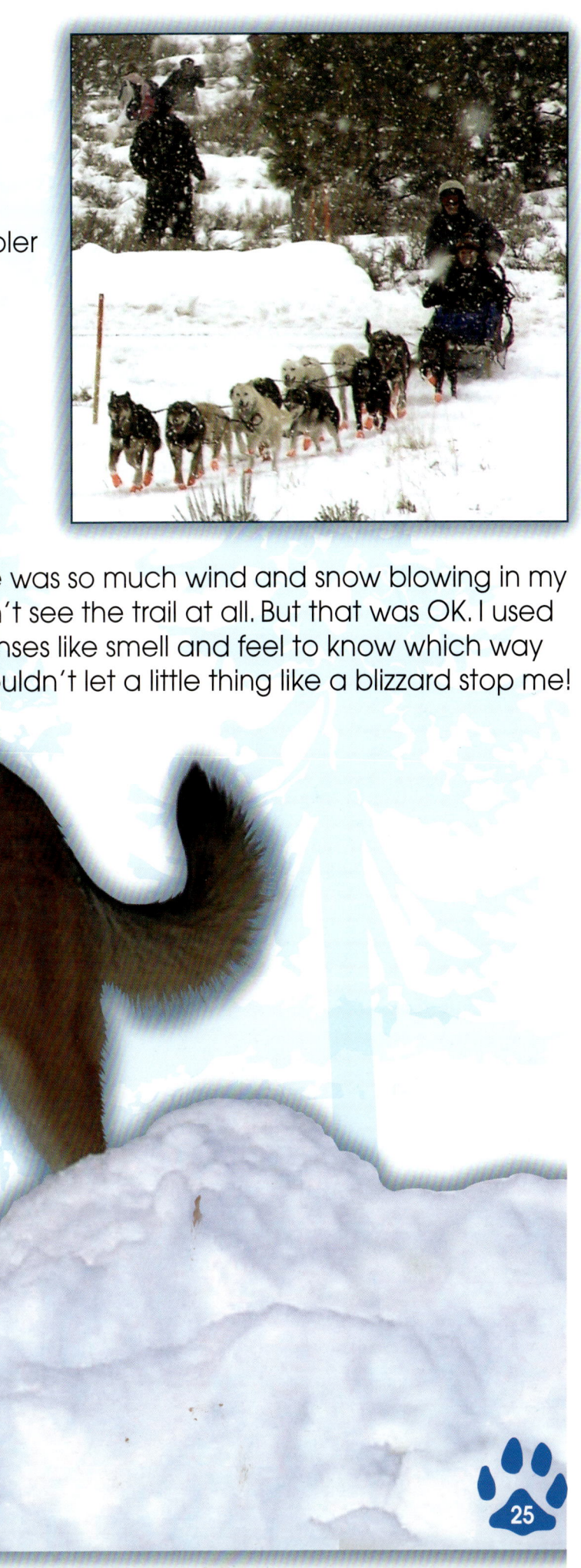

Once there was so much wind and snow blowing in my face I couldn't see the trail at all. But that was OK. I used my other senses like smell and feel to know which way to go. I wouldn't let a little thing like a blizzard stop me!

CHALLENGES

I ran and pulled like I was born to do and loved every minute of it. In each race, I showed Mom Liz I was healthy and strong and smart.

Until one awful day.

I enjoyed meat and warm soup and cozy straw to sleep on at the second rest stop during one of the races. Everything was great.

But when I woke up later that night, my foot hurt. It was the one with the toe I broke a long time ago. It hurt so bad that I couldn't finish the race, even though I wanted to.

Did You Know?
- Many distance races are a continuous format, meaning the teams rest and run alternately both day and night.
- When the dog team stops to rest at a checkpoint, they are given straw to sleep on, examined by race vets, and fed and tended to by their musher.
- The dogs always get more rest during a stop than the musher. The musher takes care of their team before their own needs, and then gets up earlier than the dogs to get them ready to leave as soon as it is time to go.

Mom Liz and the other sled dogs finished the race without me.

After we got home, Mom Liz and I went to the vets a lot. They gave me medicine for pain and cut my toenail very short to see if that would help. It didn't. Mom Liz took me to one of the best doggie foot vets in the United States. The doctor said the toe I broke long a time ago as a puppy did not heal right, after all.

I had a bunch of operations to fix my toe, but they didn't work either. Finally, the experts agreed it would be better for me if they cut off my bad toe completely.

After that, it was up to me to see if I could make my foot work with just three toes.

Mom Liz would rub my foot and put medicine on it. I had to stay home and take care of my foot for a whole year.

All the other sled dogs got to train and run in races, but not me.

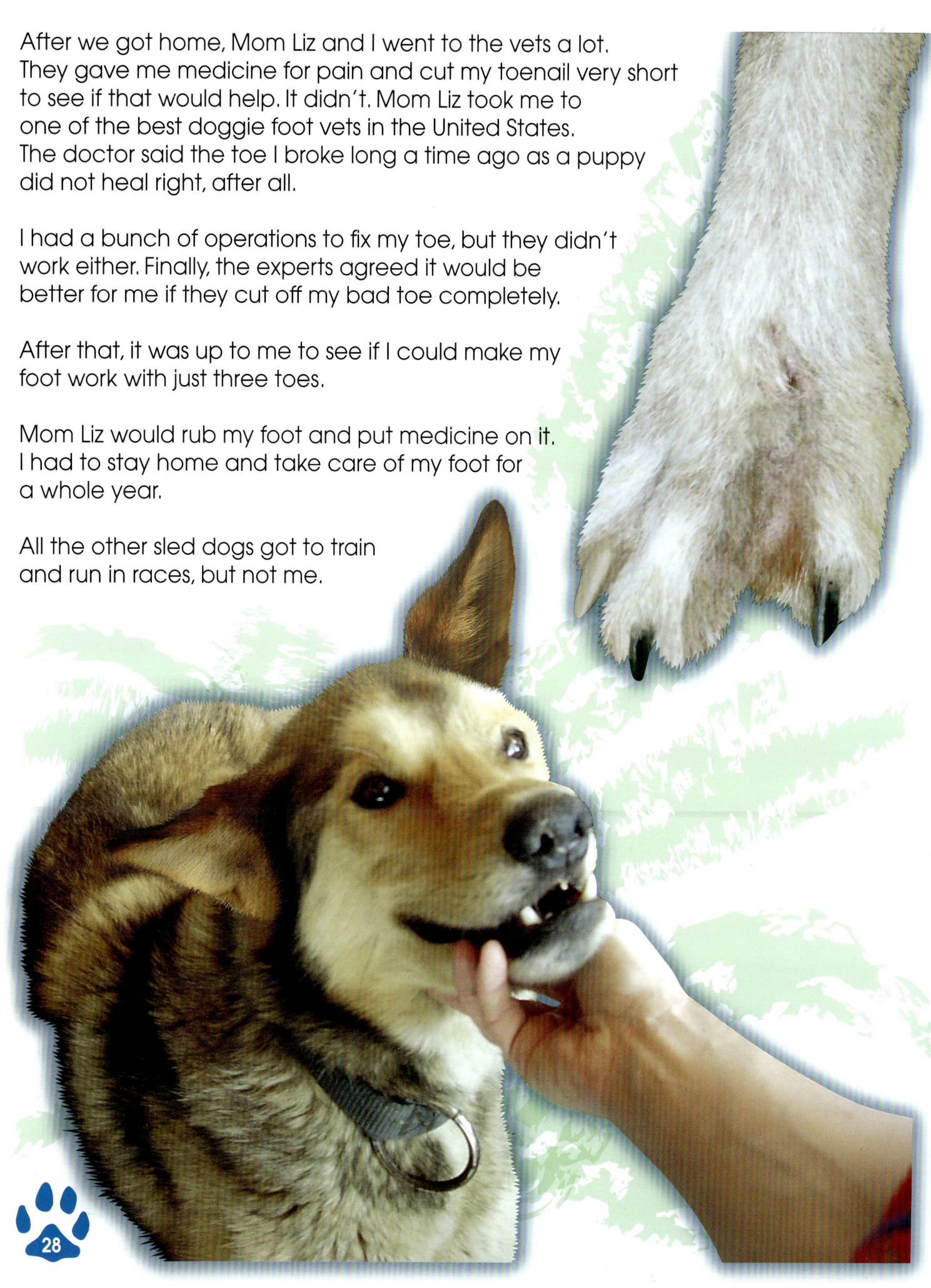

While I had all those operations on my foot, I never forgot about my destiny to be a sled dog and to be part of the dream Mom Liz had to be a musher in the Iditarod.

Mom Liz didn't forget, either. Every once in a while she would let me run with the team, but she was not happy when she could see my foot was sore.

Of course, I still wanted to GO all of the time, but Mom Liz left me at home. And it was just one year until the big race, the Iditarod!

Every time I had a chance, I put my heart into doing my very best. Because I loved to run and pull, I was eager to go in spite of my foot.

Did You Know?
- Sled dogs train thousands of miles, and run in many shorter races to get ready for a marathon race like Iditarod.
- For months in advance, the musher organizes supplies and gear for the team, making sure they are well-prepared for each stop and section of the trail.
- Mushers also must ready themselves physically and mentally for whatever challenges they might face.

Often I tried too hard and my foot would hurt so much I couldn't walk on it for a couple of days.

I CAN RUN ON THREE LEGS!
I showed Mom Liz.

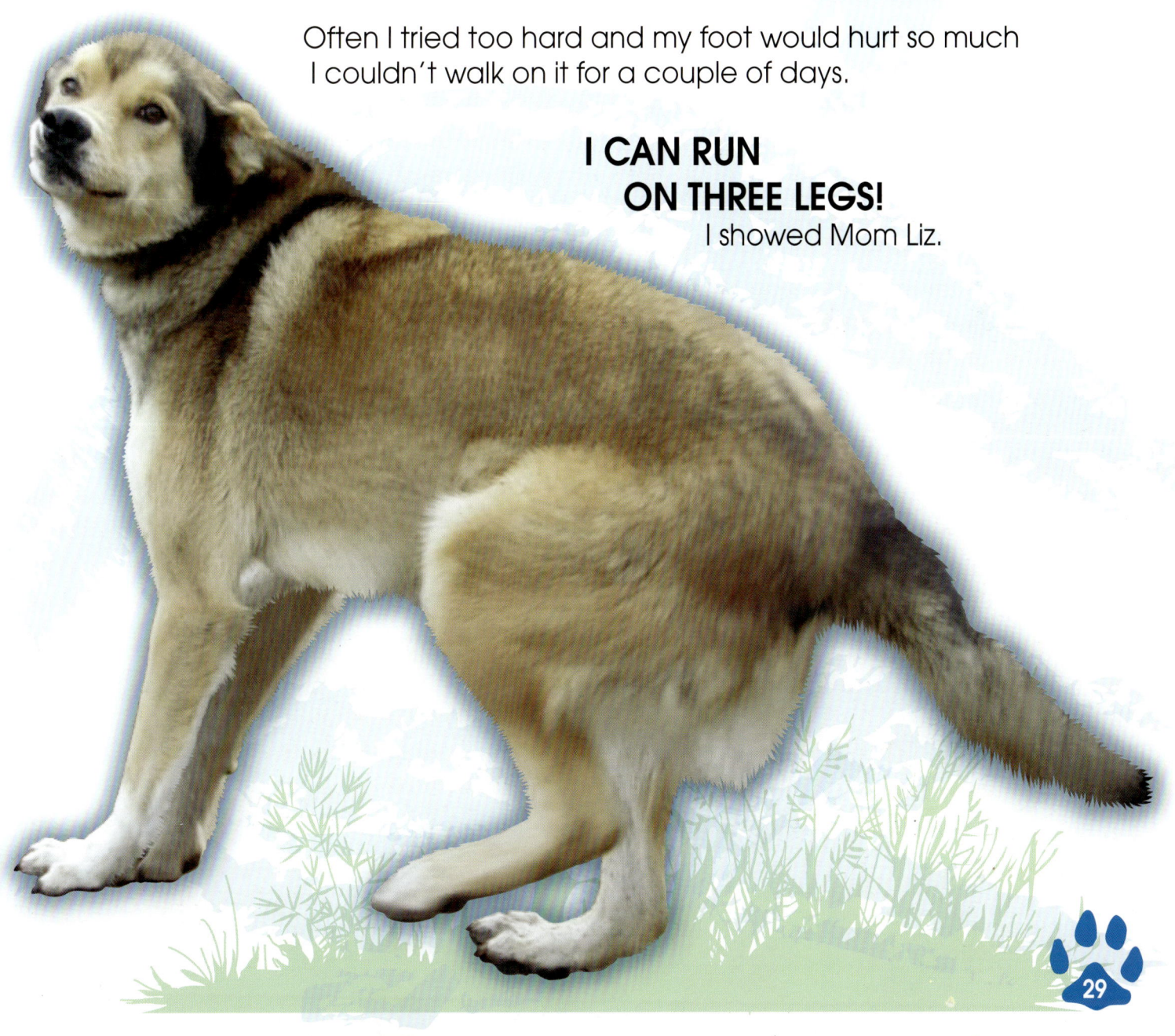

But when I did that, Mom Liz would take my harness off and tell me to rest. We didn't know what to do next.

Then, one of our friends gave us some good advice. She told Liz, **"You and Crimp worked so hard to overcome the problems you've had with his toe. He deserves a chance to try out for your Iditarod team. If Crimp wants it enough, he will figure out how to use his damaged foot."**

Of course, I really wanted to be part of the team that would run in the Iditarod. I knew I had to show Mom Liz I was healthy and strong enough to be on the team going to race in Alaska.

Whenever Mom Liz came to my place in the yard, I jumped up and looked into her eyes. I told her I was going to get better and that it didn't matter if I had a dent in my nose and a foot with three toes instead of four.

PLEASE JUST TAKE ME ALONG! I barked.

Did You Know?
- Teams start the Iditarod with a maximum of 16 dogs.
- Some large kennels have over 200 dogs of various ages and experience levels.
- Liz's kennel had a total of 26 dogs from which to choose the starting team.
- The dog teams continually practice to stay mentally sharp and to keep in shape before big races.

Mom Liz understood how much I wanted to be on the Iditarod team. **"Crimp, you showed me you are a great lead dog and teammate. I won't leave you behind. You deserve a chance just like all the others to earn a place on the Iditarod team."**

Our whole kennel traveled to Alaska for our last chance to practice and show Mom Liz what we could do.

All of the dogs worked hard, but the ones who would be chosen for the team had to be the **best**!

The more we ran, the better my foot felt, and I was able to keep up with the other dogs. I learned I could run and pull like everybody else, even without having a perfect sled dog body.

The days flew by, just like our feet over the trail.

We ran in a couple races in Alaska before the big one. One time during a race, it was dark and snowing so hard we couldn't see anything. Mom Liz yelled **"Whoa!"** so she could figure out where to go next.

Suddenly, we heard the sound of snowmobiles. Just then we realized we had stopped while crossing a snowmobile trail. The next moment, one of the snowmobiles hit me so hard I landed on the hood!

For a while, everything was confusing and the rest of the team just wanted to run away. Mom Liz gathered us up and made us feel better.

Then Mom Liz found the brass snap she uses to hook my line to the rest of the team. It was broken in half!

Mom Liz replaced it with a new snap, and we went on our way.

Did You Know?
- *Trails in Alaska are wilderness trails, meaning they are kept open by being used and are generally not groomed.*
- *Trails in races are posted with trail markers, pieces of wooden lathe with orange paint and reflective tape on the top. They are stuck in the snow banks on the side of the trail for the teams to follow.*
- *Mushers can see the markers easily during the day with the orange paint, and the reflective tape shines in the musher's headlamp light at night.*
- *The lead dogs follow the trail in difficult conditions by the scent and by how the trail feels under their feet.*

The whole team got extra food and rest that night. Mom Liz and the experts checked me out especially, to make sure I was OK.

After the race, Mom Liz took me to the vet for a check-up right away. I had some bruises and was a little sore, but that was all.

Mom Liz carries the broken snap with her all the time as a reminder of how **lucky** we both were that day!

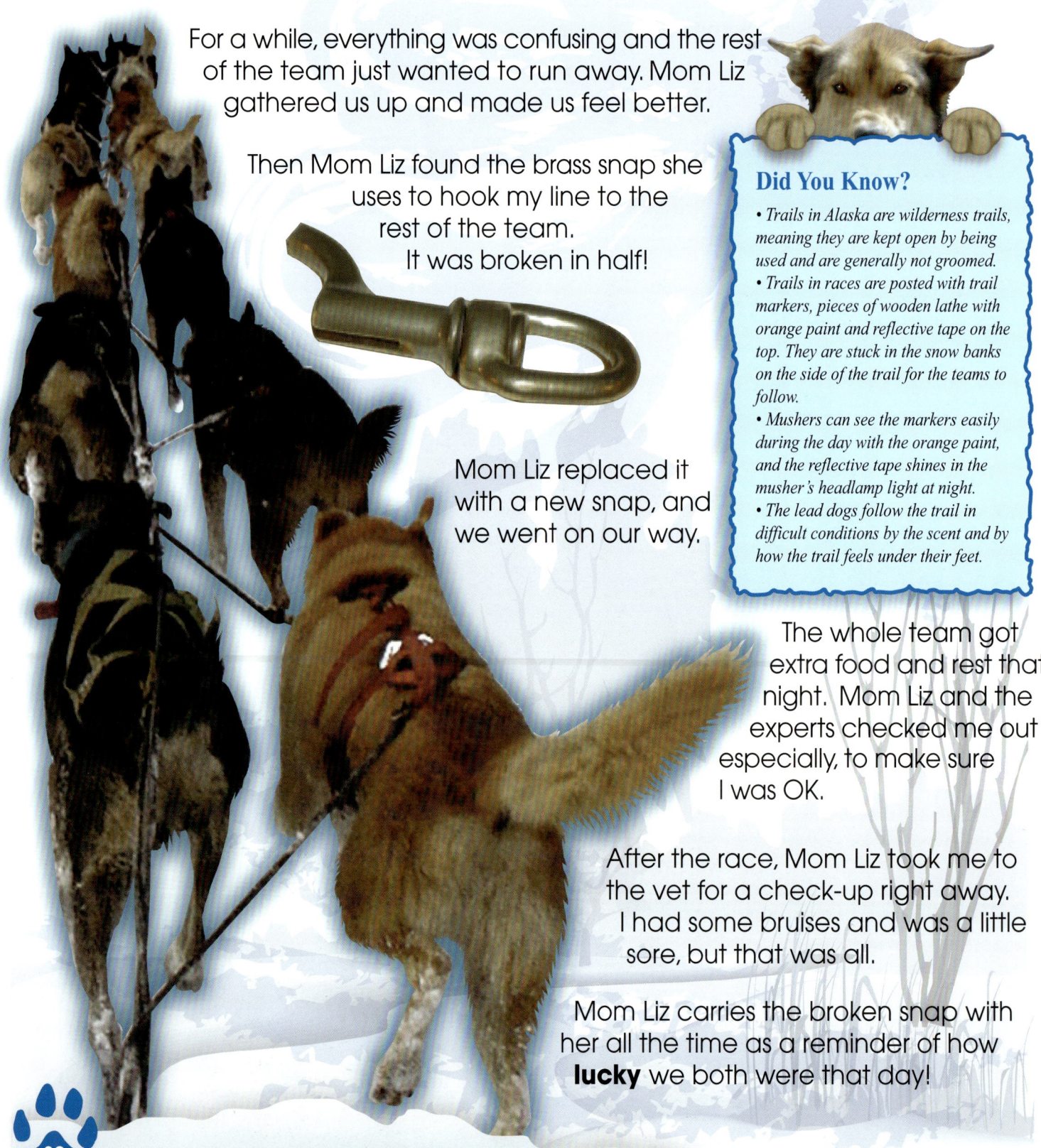

THE IDITAROD TEAM

At last the day came for Mom Liz to pick the 16 sled dogs that would run on her Iditarod team. I felt great and had done my best.

Even so, I was nervous as I saw Mom Liz come into the dog yard with some brand-new collars. Each collar had a name on it for the dogs she had selected for the big race.

PLEASE! PLEASE! PICK ME!! I barked.

I watched as she put new collars on Sinclair, Tie, Shasta, Summer and a bunch of the other dogs.

When Mom Liz came my way, she had just a few collars left…

I REALLY WANT TO GO! I barked.

Mom Liz looked at me.

I stopped barking and listened.

"Crimp, you earned your place on the Iditarod team with your heart and courage and confidence. I believe in you because you want this so much and you proved to me you can do it."

I MADE IT! I AM PART OF THE IDITAROD TEAM!!

And now it is March 1, 2008, and I'm wriggling with joy in my new collar. I don't think anything can be any better than this moment. I watch Mom Liz harness and put booties on all the other sled dogs, and when she gets to me...

I'M IN THE LEAD ON THE VERY FIRST DAY OF THE 2008 IDITAROD RACE!

AND WE HIT THE TRAIL!

In case you wondered...

Crimp and Mom Liz and the team completed the 2008 Iditarod Sled Dog Race of 1,150 miles in 14 days, 19 hours, 51 minutes and 27 seconds.

They all had a blast!

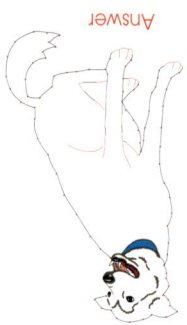

Connect the dots and draw Crimp

Lessons from the Sled Dogs

Crimp does not perceive what he did as heroic, or courageous, or anything out of the ordinary. This is one of his most powerful lessons—how much can be accomplished by knowing where you want to go and giving your best to get there, regardless of roadblocks and setbacks. Crimp was a constant source of inspiration to me as I worked toward the Iditarod dream. After all, if he can do it, and want it, with every fiber of his being…how could I do less?

How could I let him down?

Other lessons Crimp continues to teach are those of the essence of sled dogs: Be in the moment; Trust; Patience; Focus. He doesn't have any idea of the example he sets or the inspiration he provides—Crimp is simply in sync with his being and purpose. He is happy and fulfilled…and always ready for more.

I continue to help Crimp make those lessons available for everyone looking to enrich their own lives and possibilities. I am partnering with Barb Schaefer, a mushing friend who is also nurtured by her dogs, to develop Life…Through Dogs ℠. This venture focuses on helping folks unleash their full potential in life. We accomplish this by sharing the many life lessons learned from Crimp and his fellow sled dogs in a variety of ways: talks, coaching, hands-on clinics with the dogs, adventure experiences, and information products such as this book, to name but a few. A key tenet of Life…Through Dogs is that dogs mirror and reflect, without judgment, how harmoniously we are living at any given moment. We can best learn about life, and ourselves, through these wonderful teachers. More information is available on the Life…Through Dogs website, www.lifethroughdogs.com, as well as Crimp's own website, www.crimponby.com.

As we prepared for Iditarod 2008, my co-author Jan invariably reminded me the real victory was getting to the starting line. I needed to learn that lesson. Crimp already knew.

Liz Parrish

Crimp! On-By!! Copies and More Information

Please send me the following:

Number of Copies	Unit Price	Total Price
_____	$12.95	_____
	Shipping:	_____
	Purchase TOTAL:	_____

Please send me FREE information on:

__ Speaking/Appearances   __ Coaching   __ Clinics

Name: _____

Billing Address: _____

City, State, Zip: _____

(If different) Shipping Address: _____

City, State, Zip: _____

Email: _____

Phone: _____
(Your contact information is safe with us – we will NOT sell or rent our customer information.)

Shipping: US Domestic – $4.00 first book, $2.50 each additional book
Please contact us for international shipping charges.

(Please make checks payable to Life Through Dogs.)

Online: www.crimponby.com, *order securely online*

Fax orders by Credit Card: 866-294-4213 • **Phone orders by Credit Card:** 541-892-3639

Postal Mail: Life Through Dogs, Liz Parrish, P.O. Box 498, Ft. Klamath, OR 97626, USA

Telephone: 541-892-3639 • **Email:** contact@lifethroughdogs.com

Please call or email for quantity discounts.